A LOOK AT EARTH'S ROCKS

WHAT IS THE ROCK CYCLE?

BY FRANCES NAGLE

Gareth Stevens PUBLISHING

CRASHCOURSE

Please visit our website, www.garethstevens.com. For a free color catalog of all our high-quality books, call toll free 1-800-542-2595 or fax 1-877-542-2596.

Library of Congress Cataloging-in-Publication Data

Names: Nagle, Frances, 1959-
Title: What is the rock cycle? / Frances Nagle.
Description: New York : Gareth Stevens Publishing, [2018] | Series: A look at Earth's rocks | Includes index.
Identifiers: LCCN 2016040623| ISBN 9781482460193 (pbk. book) | ISBN 9781482460209 (6 pack) | ISBN 9781482460216 (library bound book)
Subjects: LCSH: Petrology--Juvenile literature. | Geology--Juvenile literature. | Rocks--Juvenile literature.
Classification: LCC QE432.2 .N34 2018 | DDC 552--dc23
LC record available at https://lccn.loc.gov/2016040623

First Edition

Published in 2018 by
Gareth Stevens Publishing
111 East 14th Street, Suite 349
New York, NY 10003

Designer: Samantha DeMartin
Editor: Kristen Nelson

Photo credits: Series background winnond/Shutterstock.com; caption box Edhar Shvets/Shutterstock.com; cover, p. 1 Ammit Jack/Shutterstock.com; p. 5 (top right) Kenneth Keifer/Shutterstock.com; p. 5 (bottom) nineyoii/Shutterstock.com; p. 5 (top left) Budkov Denis/Shutterstock.com; p. 7 Naeblys/Shutterstock.com; p. 9 (top) Peter Hermes Furian/Shutterstock.com; p. 9 (bottom) Adwo/Shutterstock.com; p. 11 JTB Photo/Universal Images Group/Getty Images; p. 13 A_Lesik/Shutterstock.com; p. 15 BarryTuck/Shutterstock.com; p. 17 jack0m/Getty Images; p. 19 (top) Matthijs Wetterauw/Shutterstock.com; p. 19 (bottom) Artesia Wells/Shutterstock.com; p. 21 Sekar B/Shutterstock.com; p. 23 Lindsay Douglas/Shutterstock.com; p. 25 My Good Images/Shutterstock.com; p. 27 (mountains) Wolfgang Berroth/Shutterstock.com; p. 27 (rock face) Dan Kosmayer/Shutterstock.com; p. 27 (pebbles) Birgitta Kullman/Shutterstock.com; p. 29 Wellford Tiller/Shutterstock.com; p. 30 Spencer Sutton/Getty Images.

Printed in the United States of America

CPSIA compliance information: Batch #CS17GS: For further information contact Gareth Stevens, New York, New York at 1-800-542-2595.

CONTENTS

Words in the glossary appear in **bold** type the first time they are used in the text.

THE MYSTERY OF ROCK

Earth is made of rock. Rock forms naturally. Until the 1700s, scientists didn't know how that happened. Then, a scientist came up with a new idea: Earth's rock has been slowly forming, breaking down, and re-forming in the same way for a long time.

MAKE THE GRADE

This idea, presented by John Hutton, is used in a scientific **model** called the rock cycle. A cycle is a series of steps that happens over and over again.

THE LAYERS

Earth has four **layers**: a hard outer crust, a hot mantle, an outer core, and an inner core. The crust and the upper part of the mantle are called the lithosphere. The lithosphere is where the rock cycle mostly happens.

EARTH'S LAYERS

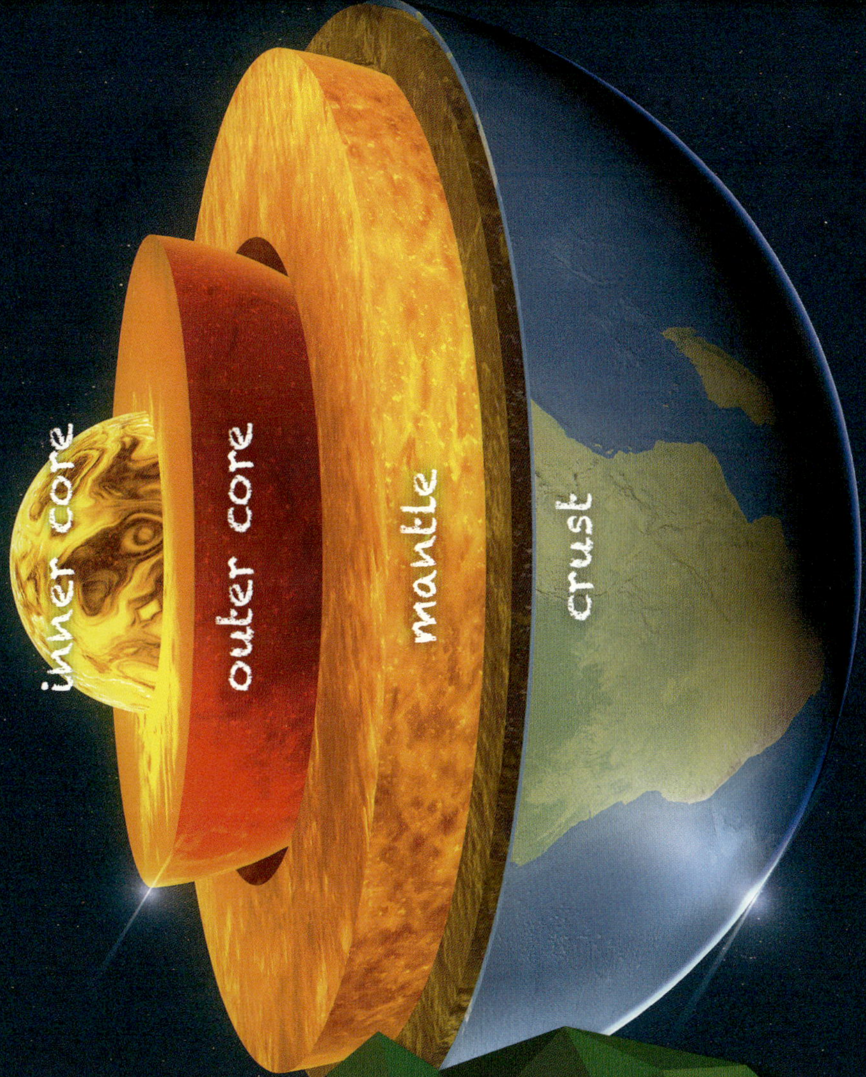

MAKE THE GRADE

The crust is what we most often see—but it's a very small part of Earth's rock!

The lithosphere is made up of big pieces of rock called tectonic plates. These plates move! They slide past one another, run into each other, and slip under and over each other. These movements cause parts of the rock cycle to occur.

EARTH'S TECTONIC PLATES

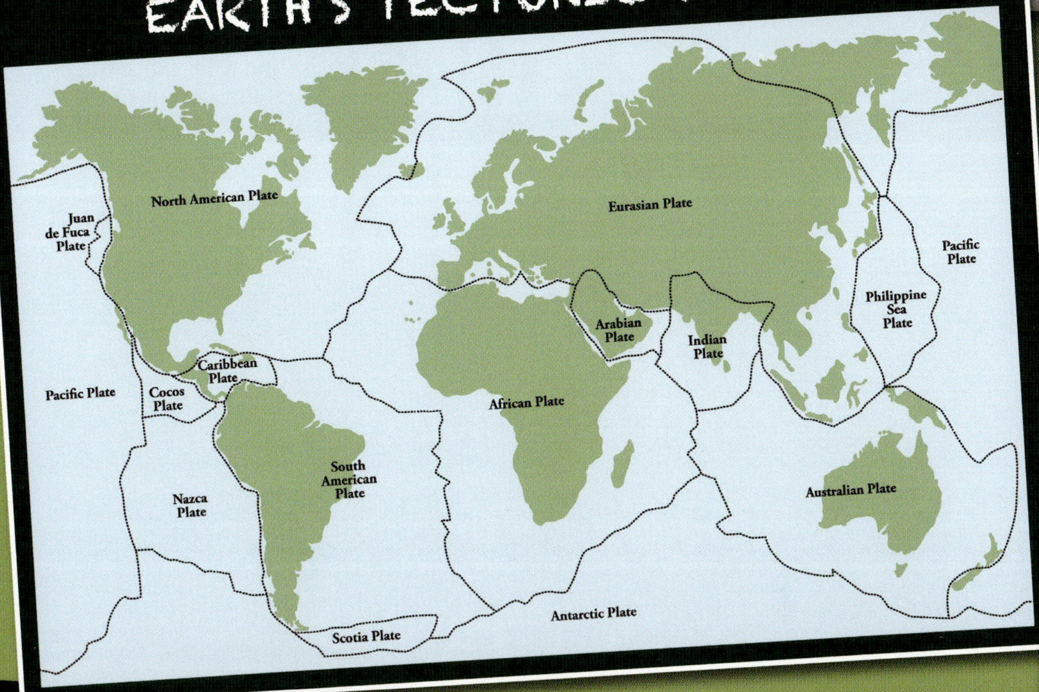

MAKE THE GRADE

Scientists who study the history and form of Earth are called geologists.

START THE CYCLE: WEATHERING

The rock cycle starts with weathering, or the breaking down of rock. **Physical** weathering includes wind and water breaking down rock. Water may also freeze inside rock and cause it to crack. Animals can cause weathering by digging at soft rock, too.

MAKE THE GRADE

Chemical weathering is when water mixed with **minerals** flows into rock, causing it to get softer and break down.

Weathering creates sediment. When that sediment moves, it's called erosion. Sediment is often carried by wind or water. **Gravity** can also be part of erosion, such as pulling loose rock down a mountainside in a rockslide.

MAKE THE GRADE

Sediment includes sand, soil, small stones, and any bits of rock that have broken off from other rock.

MAKING SEDIMENTARY ROCK

Once sediment settles in a place, it can become rock! Matter, including other sediment, buries it. The **pressure** on the buried sediment builds up. Water flows into the open spaces and leaves behind minerals that bind sediment together. This forms sedimentary rock!

MAKE THE GRADE

Sedimentary rock often forms in layers. Lower layers are older than those above them.

METAMORPHIC ROCK

Rock existing on Earth's surface, such as sedimentary rock, may be pushed deep underground as the tectonic plates move. The heat and pressure rise. The rock has to change in order to remain **stable**.

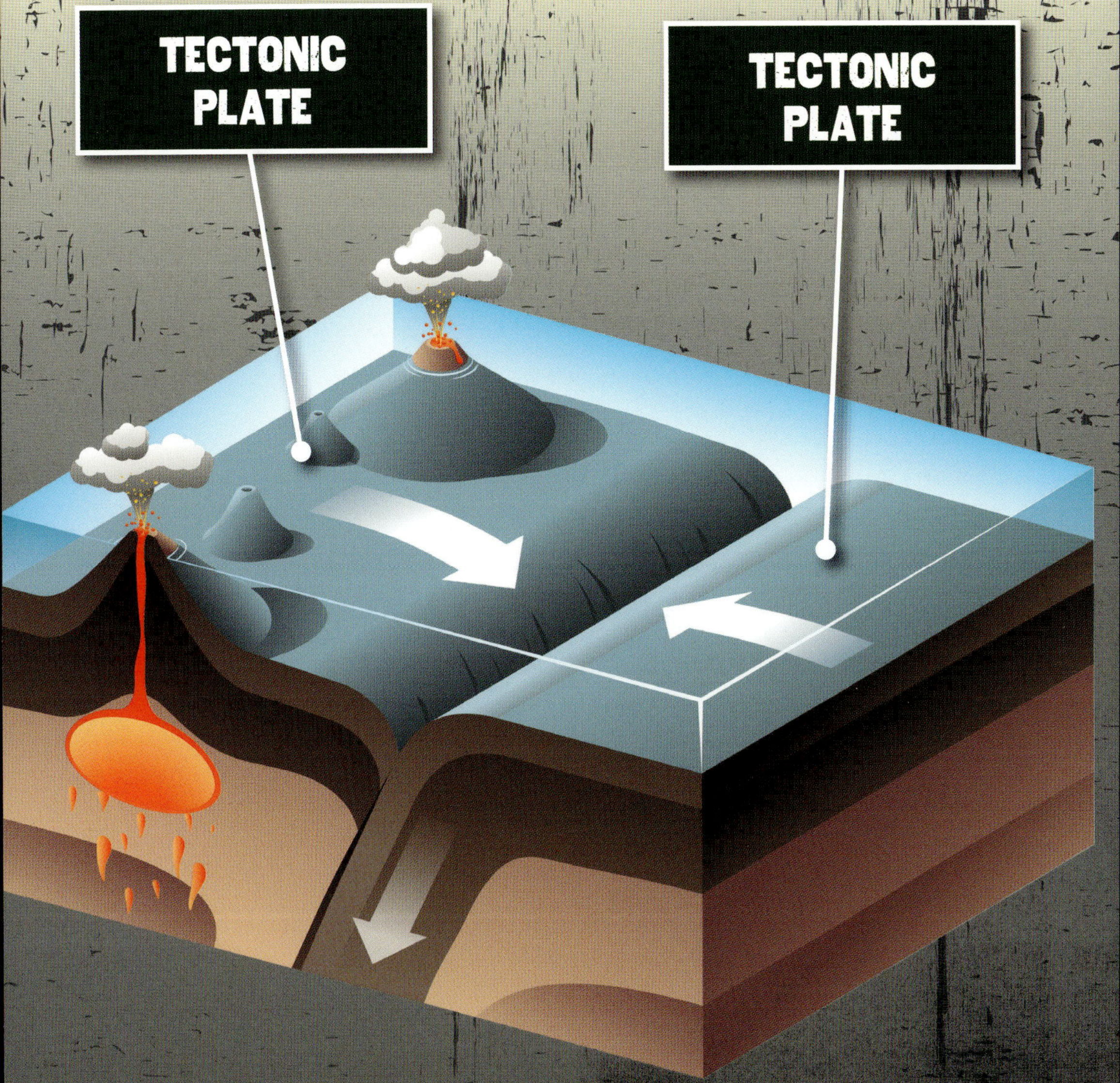

MAKE THE GRADE

The existing rock that's facing new conditions is called "parent rock."

When the chemical makeup of rock changes because of new conditions, it forms metamorphic rock. Any kind of rock can become metamorphic rock—even other metamorphic rock!

MAKE THE GRADE

The minerals in the parent rock play a big part in what kind of metamorphic rock will form.

HOT ROCK

When rock is pushed even deeper into Earth, it can get so hot, the rock melts! When rock is liquid underground, it's called magma. When this hot, liquid rock rises and cools, it forms igneous rock.

MAKE THE GRADE

When magma reaches Earth's surface, it's called lava.

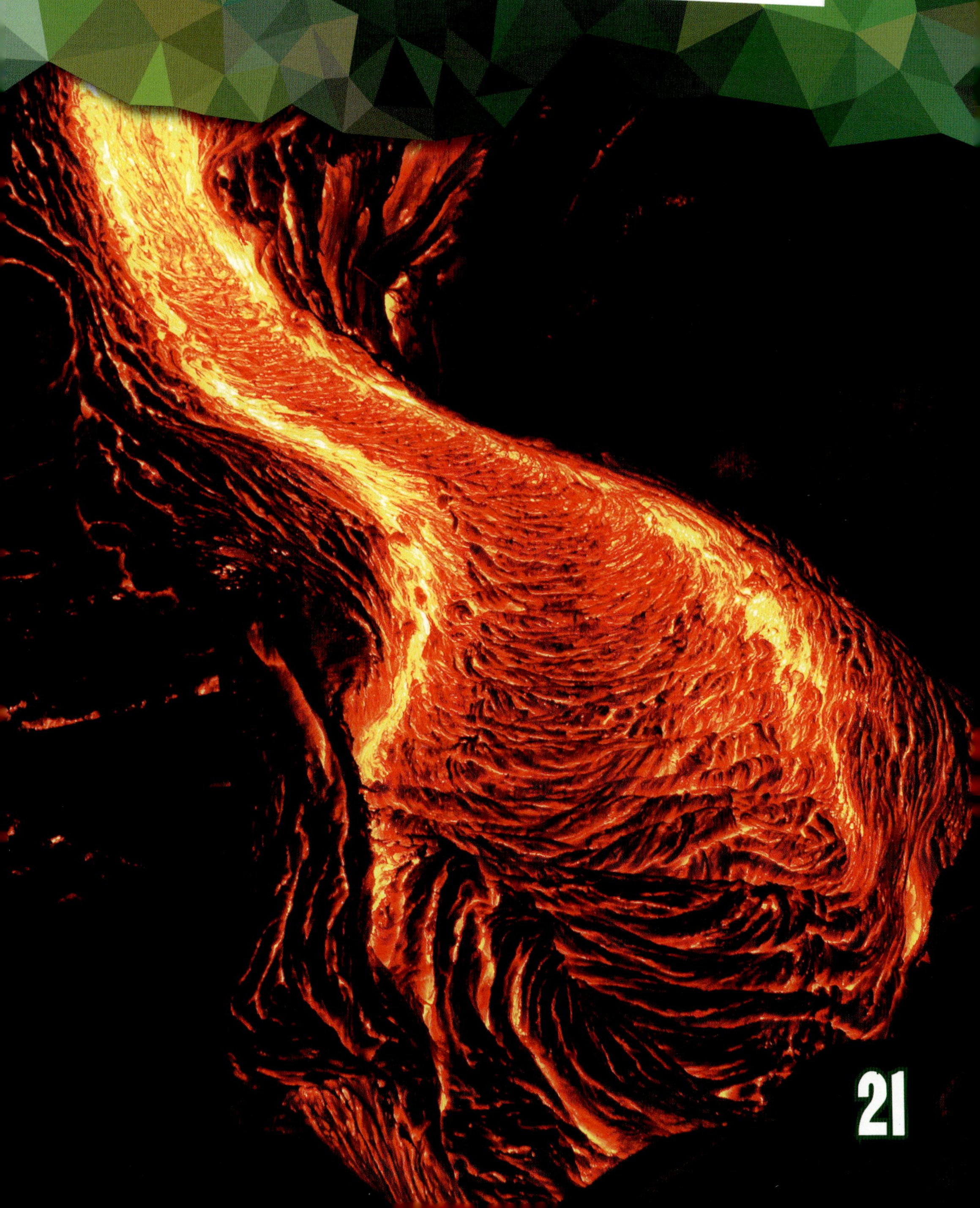

Igneous rock can form underground as magma flows into pockets and tunnels below Earth's surface. Or igneous rock can form when lava reaches Earth's surface and cools. It may burst from a crack in Earth's crust called a volcano!

MAKE THE GRADE

The only way for new rock to form is through igneous **processes**.

UPLIFT

Just as tectonic plates move some rock deeper underground, their movement also raises some rock higher! This is called uplift. Uplift is what forms mountains and hills. When these are created, rock faces weathering again. The rock cycle begins anew!

MAKE THE GRADE

Without uplift, the rock cycle would stop after a time. Mountains would wear away completely!

ROCK GOES ON

The rock cycle is more than just a scientific model. It's an ongoing process with no real beginning or end. It's been happening since Earth formed, and it's going on right now!

MAKE THE GRADE

The water cycle is another scientific model that shows how water moves around Earth.

Geologists can figure out how old rock is and what kind it is by looking at its chemical makeup. Using this knowledge, they've learned that Earth is about 4.6 billion years old! That's a long time for the rock cycle to have been going on!

MAKE THE GRADE

As geologists study rock, they discover fossils. These are the hardened marks or remains of past animals and plants that are found in rock.

THE ROCK CYCLE

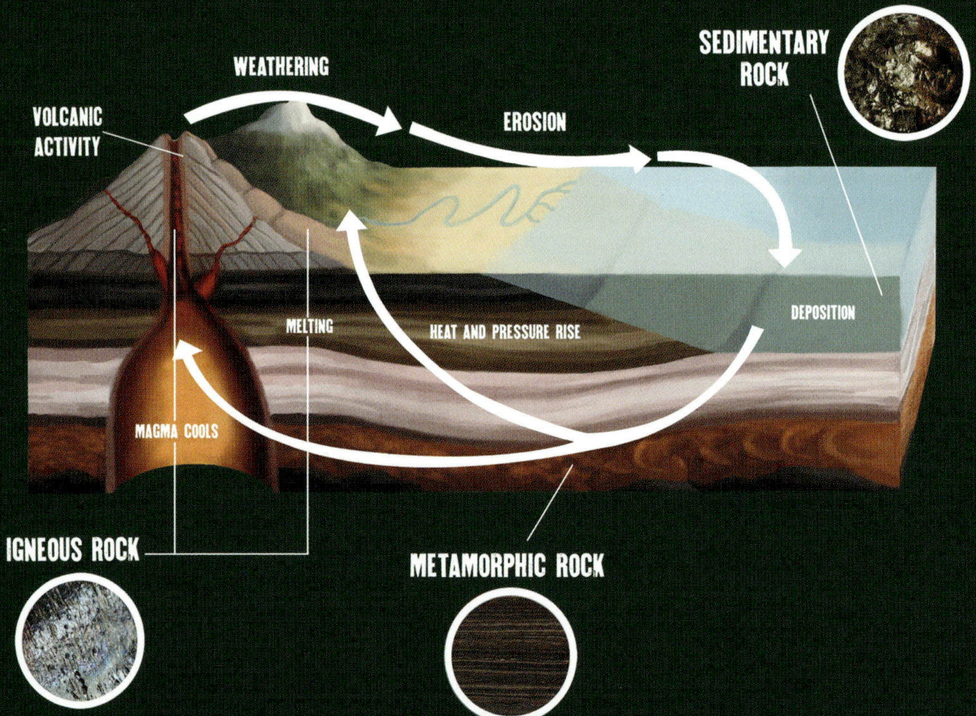

GLOSSARY

chemical: having to do with matter that can be mixed with other matter to cause changes

gravity: the force that pulls objects toward Earth's center

layer: one thickness of something lying over or under another

mineral: matter in the ground that forms rocks

model: a way of explaining something that occurs in the natural world

physical: having to do with matter

pressure: the application of force

process: a set of steps

stable: not likely to change suddenly or greatly

FOR MORE INFORMATION

BOOKS

Conklin, Wendy. *Earth's Cycles*. Huntington Beach, CA: Teacher Created Materials, 2016.

Lindeen, Mary. *Investigating the Rock Cycle*. Minneapolis, MN: Lerner Publications, 2016.

WEBSITES

Rock Cycle for Kids

www.dkfindout.com/us/earth/rock-cycle/

Explore the rock cycle further on this website!

Publisher's note to educators and parents: Our editors have carefully reviewed these websites to ensure that they are suitable for students. Many websites change frequently, however, and we cannot guarantee that a site's future contents will continue to meet our high standards of quality and educational value. Be advised that students should be closely supervised whenever they access the Internet.

INDEX